bodies,
and other haunted houses

bodies,
and other haunted houses

SL Grange

SEREN

Seren is the book imprint of
Poetry Wales Press Ltd
Suite 6, 4 Derwen Road, Bridgend,
Wales, CF31 1LH

www.serenbooks.com
facebook.com/SerenBooks
twitter@SerenBooks

The right of SL Grange to be identified as
the author of this work has been asserted in accordance
with the Copyright, Designs and Patents Act, 1988.

© SL Grange 2022.

ISBN: 978-1-78172-681-5

A CIP record for this title is available from the British Library.

All rights reserved. No part of this publication may be reproduced,
stored in a retrieval system, or transmitted at any time or by any means,
electronic, mechanical, photocopying, recording or otherwise without
the prior permission of the copyright holder.

The publisher acknowledges the financial assistance
of the Books Council of Wales.

Printed in Bembo by 4Edge Ltd.

Contents

7	Queer Times
8	Cold Ham
9	Where are we going, Mary Frith?
10	Ritual for
12	She Protests
13	Safe words
14	Service
15	This morning I
16	Resharpen your weapons
17	White poem
18	This shit is killing you, too, however much more softly, you stupid mother fucker, you know?
19	After Sappho
20	Desire is a ghost
22	Daughter
23	The Glory
24	Malkin Tower
29	Pockets
30	Whales at night
31	Under
32	Sun-return
34	*Acknowledgements*

Queer Times

All of this has been written before,
in the godless corners at the back of churches,
in the dirt of cotton-fields-corn-fields-battle-fields-
in the dirt, any way.

Scratched in the timber or plaster
of our small and smoke-dark shelters,

in lipstick on powder-room mirrors
and on bus timetables in crude biro too.

We wrote furtively,
our fingertips already see-through,
the quick of our nails splintering as we went-
there was never much time.

Words, and sometimes just noises –
desperate for any kind of memorial at all;

a heap of crumbs swept into a corner
would do – dry and stale and far too late.

We pushed our hands and feet into wet cement,
fucking off the builders,
cut crude hearts into the bark of trees
with blunt knives,

squatted over rare snowfalls
to write our names in pure piss,

lined up grains of rice on café table tops,
pointing the way to something.

We pressed our torsos, naked, against shop windows
at night to leave a greasy form behind,
filling in the missing parts by licking the glass
at the apex of our thighs,

mouths gaping just enough to let out a little air.

To let in a little, too.

Cold Ham

The parachute opened
        precisely four seconds too late,
cutting off in abrupt vertigo
the rush of air past my ears,
leaving a ringing silence
in which I could hear
not my soft, lingering breath,
but the keening I didn't know
–until then–
I could make.

As the treetops, anthills and charging horses hurtled up to meet me
I saw the picnic you had spread out;
a perfect pie,
        lemonade, cool in an earthenware jug.

Four seconds too late
jug, lemonade, crisp pastry, my ribcage.

At the moment of impact:
        thigh bones
                pushing up and out at my throat.

Where are we going, Mary Frith[1]?

White sheets lifting
in the February wind,
winding round our knees and ankles–
the rough wood of the scaffold
snagging
against the callouses of our palms

The crowd lift our feet
one by one up the steps
as if our bare soles belonged
to their cupped hands

Priests know how to whip
and split us,
scalding the shame on
with holy water
flung from a distance

But they don't know
where we're going,
our scars fresh
blistered
and our mouths wet
with penitence

(We slip our feet through woollen breeches,
tie our points up neat as a Sunday prayer
pit pat
Oh, and we will chop our hair
clean off
at the chin,
our breasts bound
in white sheets
winding)

---

1. Mary Frith alias Mal or Moll Cutpurse was a cross-dressing performer and criminal living in London between 1588 and 1659.

Ritual for

Take handfuls of paprika and salt.
Walk to the end of the road or path or stream.
Raise your fists to the sky.

In your stomach is a bird's nest.
The eggs hatched long time back.
The shells cracked and softly glowing blue.

Lie in the middle of the road the path the stream.
With cut grass and flesh in your palms.
Raise your fists to the sky.

In your throat is a drum
taut and humming
waiting for your fists to come down

tarmac eyelids tongue gravel
leaves gutter crisp packets
tarmac eyelids tongue gravel

leaves gutter crisp packets.
The inside of your cut lip.
On your knees.

To standing or to chair.
Fill your stomach with cut grass.
Soles on earth.

Fists in air.
Look in their eyes.
Paprika handfuls.

Reach in to their bird nest guts.
Crack the eggs.
Beat the drum in your throat.

Beat the drum.
Throw the salt into the road/path/stream.
Bring down your fists.

Beat the drum in your throat
beat the drum
birds fly birds fly out.

She Protests

Such a tall girl
in the middle of the crowd.

This is why she frowns,
picks up the pace.

Someone give her a placard so
she has something to do with her hands,

something to use when it becomes
necessary to swat away the damn flies,

borrowed words to shout as
she leans her long self down.

Mouth to mouth.

Spitting into their faces for a change,
learning how long her reach really is,

throwing punches
as chicken bones to jackals-

Why feed them anything more than
what you don't want anyway?

Safe words

Ball the socks
And place them in the drawer
Count them

Fold the underpants very carefully
(the intimacy of the cloth)

Lean your hips into the side of the bed

(you can let go now)

Curled into the shower tray
Clench your body like a fist
Make tea make tea

Arrange the biros in a line
Fold the napkins very carefully
(the intimacy of the cloth)

Press the air into the side of the lungs

(you can let go now)

The surgical gloves
       The surgical gowns
The surgical precision of where they left the grit (inside)

Curled in the shower tray in the clenched fist in the balled sock in the intimate cloth

(you can let go now)

You can put on your heavy boots
Where the small stones sit
Walk to the end of the pier
(and back)

Unsteady air in your clenched fist

(you can let go now)

Service

There was one hymn the deputy head-
mistress refused to sing,
linen-fold panelling resounding
around her steady silent gaze.

In cold classrooms later she explained
we shouldn't be coerced
into making promises just because
they were sung and sewn in verse.

Young girls show so much promise,
traders at our market stalls-
to love for ever, do our best,
     – or to never tell a soul.

Unfolding as we grow older
the fabric of the lies we told,
we unpick the stitches of our oaths,
cut out unwanted syllables; so

I vow to thee my cunt
All earthly things above
Entire and whole and perfect
The service of my love.

This morning I

let a red admiral out at the window
poured boiling water over the ants

placed a single pink petal on my tongue
and let it sit there –

this is how I meet you
petal-tongued mass-murderer

in the evening if you ask me
how was your day

I will lift the wine glass high
the small lines of my fingerprints

lying on the surface
and ask you if you would like some herbal tea

and put the kettle on again
filled with fresh water now

boiling against the stainless steel
I open my mouth –

butterflies and scalding steam
butterflies and scalding steam

Resharpen your weapons
– *Amina of Zazzau*

Sisters, siblings,
if your blades are blunted
whet them on white collars,
ballot papers, or the railings
of private parks.

Pull sideways, like so,
across gritted surfaces;
the plinths and pointing fingers
of declamatory statues
or the belt buckles of racists,
rapists,
and the rest –
they all wear belts.

Knuckles and between teeth,
the small bones of wrists
or ankles,
the gap between pay cheques,
and the in-breath
between hey and bitch
can be good places to practice
your stroke.

Once it is sharp again
take it in the palm of your hand,
weigh it softly

and throw it far

into the sky around deportations, or towards the top floor
of those high shining towers
where the wires are easily cut,
the glass easily broken.

Glass too, makes a good blade.

White poem

This is a poem that throws everything else to the dogs
This is a poem that buys tinned tuna
Coffee
Green beans out of season
And finds the excess to be lyrical
Full of portent

This poem only cares about
Walking varnished nails
Across skin like cream
And looks out of the window
Tear ducts moistening
To see a Pepper's ghost of itself
Staring back, deeply moved

This poem has found The One
And dances with them
Under filament lightbulbs

One hand upon their lover's shoulder
The other on their lover's neck

Starting to squeeze

> This shit is killing you, too, however much more softly, you stupid motherfucker, you know?
> — Fred Moten, *The Undercommons*

My breasts are not your breasts to beat
Ba-dum
Ba-dum
They are my own soft and furious handfuls
for me alone to rip off and throw against whatever wall I choose

So, just as I am free, also, to wrap them in clean linen,
are you free
to celebrate your monthly
procession through blood, sweat and fears

What our bodies love is liberty
from each other's progress

What our bodies love is liberty
from the same blasted wasteland

To curl up with our shoulders touching against the rough bricks;
a spring compressed,
a shove.

After Sappho[2]

Take me in [ ] arms Peggy Shaw
                        [   ]Shaw
[ ] will suck your thumb wh[ ]
[   ]pro[   ]ever die.

[   ] freckled [ ]
Musc[   ]
[   ] lift and hold us to the hot bright light

On your lap [   ] heartbeats
[ ] all the queers lost [   ] fire
O[   ] danger
Of wet fingertips

[ ] suck [   ]

---

2. Inspired by Anne Carson's translations of Sappho's poetry fragments, this piece is a response to degraded VHS archive footage of Split Britches / Bloolips 1990 collaborative performance *Belle Reprieve*.

Desire is a ghost

Yes, yes, we all know that one.

A woman in lace and crinolines
who flutters ineffectually behind the brocade curtains;

A sad little flat-cap man
dripping drowned and dowdy on Shadwell stairs;

A limp white figure leaping in unrequited bellyflop
from high Gothic crenulations;

A bare-breasted boy weeping luxurious tears on the grave of Oscar Wilde,
red rose between his perfect lips;

A banging cupboard door that cannot be stopped;
A record on the turntable singing the same scratched crackle to itself;
A disembodied wail in the night;
A scrap of petticoat caught on a nail;
An incurable cough;

A clammy sweat breaking out on the forehead of an intrepid disbeliever at midnight on the upstairs landing as they pass the spare bedroom door in the dead of night on their way for a piss because actually they *can* hear a spectral child's laughter;

The wild ghosts of fauns and foxes, hunted bloody,
and the dogs that tear the flesh, roiling in guttural frantic heaves – limbs clawing, hooves jerking,
all toothed and bitten biting;

Or a kiss placed exquisitely on the nape of a warm neck,
ten years ago now
but still so present.

Desire is a ghost
Yes
Yes
Yes

Daughter

Running hard towards the edge of everything
she carried her shoes in her hands
flinging them upwards
to catch on phone lines

Destiny was not a byword for her
the end of the road no kind of border
– patrolled by stray animals and
invitations to roam

Every day began like a shout
a motion into sky
shorts patched and t-shirt grubby
with leaves fallen unnoticed

A cartwheel soul tumbling riot
always mid-air spinning into the river
having leapt the banks
with her heart on her open palms

You are waiting
to hear how she landed broken –
that fate put out a malicious foot
tripped her in the dance

No

Simply, she spins a dandelion
head always, watching
soft white seeds float
downstream with the breeze

Rainbow leggings and a forthright
little mouth ready
to grin and open tender with demands
an O of wonder, an O

The Glory

The bar has been left exactly as it was found
except some small adjustments for safety.

On the round tables
are a number of sticky marks
from rum and coke on ice
slopped over rims and fingers.

The smell is stale sweat, ancient now,
a mere hint of smoke machine tang by the stage.

We know there would once have been a tinsel curtain.
We think it may have been taken by looters
perhaps for an important burial.

One of the most surprising finds
was just the sheer quantity of glitter.
It was likely used in rituals
perhaps of rebirth or sacrifice.

If you stand still at the bar and listen
you can almost hear the cheers

for the twin half-smiles of top-surgery scars
on the man on the stage
who is taking off his clothes
to prove he survived–
if not unscathed, at least loved.

What will you order
before you take the microphone
and let the ghosts have use of your tongue?

What taste would you like in your mouth
as it fills with leather and someone else's flesh?

Malkin Tower[3]

i.

He did desire her daughter
to have his pleasure of her
denied the said
whereupon the said
in a great anger took his horse

Get out of my ground
whores and witches,
I will burn the one of you,
and hang the other
said

a brown cow of the said
upon her in the night time
in the likeness of a bear,
gaping as though
he would have wearied her

What part of her body
he would have for that use,
to go outside?

The cow died
The said horse or mare died
Two sticks across in the same field
The said
The unsaid

We denied the said
the use of our body

Nip and bite
Burn the one
Hang the other
Refuse a penny
Deny an old shirt

Begging a bowl of blue milk
Begging pins
Begging a penny
To get blood
under her arm

Day-light gate
She wanted nothing yet-

took eight teeth,
kept four to her self

ii.

One of the little secrets we have
is to look in his eyes
(we've got money in the bank)

Did you notice
my hand running over your ear?
Accept this and love this
I might pull
I might touch

Do you want to go outside?

These things are down
on the ground
Wrestling
Nip and bite

We shape our bodies in clay
We move our flesh around
in wet nights
Slide our hands down
Stand our ground
Dogs curling round our
legs, wet with mud

We pointed the finger at you
We pointed at your face
We said
Burn us hang us
Hang thyself

We don't want to discourage you
It's important that you
are ready
with some kind of leash
or line

I'm going to slip my hand in
Sliding down
You want to play?
I'll let you chase me
Good baby
I'll squeeze a little

to correct

I praise him
Yes
Another situation
In a submissive position
Looking calm
Waving paws

Gaping

iii.

Look at us
Our bodies clay-baked
by the hearths
Crumbled away
For a penny
For a bowl of milk

Who sells their soul for this
poor banquet
of want and bare threads?
These dreams
Bear-wearied
Crumbling clay dreams
As each fades
they languish for a year
or three or four days
then the said die

Our ribs, below our arms
Below our breasts
Four-score years
Our sight robbed
by dogs, by hares
Spitting fire

The rain drips through
the fir needles
and into the cracks
in our reverend fathers
We go stark mad for eight weeks
We walk the old paths
between men
between rage, displeasure
and a map of our bodies
Enclosed

Our eyes one lower
than the other
Our stink and our old hands

that crumble and
mis-shape
with the long years
Of your fucking
laundry and kneading
and hard floors

and rough wood
Your demands
Your bargains and
what we sold long before
any white foal
or brown dog
or bear
stopped us in the woods and
gave the honour of a soul-
Saw the possibility
of this sacred
little bright piece
waiting

Do you want to go outside?
It's important that you are ready

---

3. Much of the text of the first canto is taken from Thomas Potts' account of the Pendle witch trials of 1612; *The Wonderfull Discoverie of Witches in the Countie of Lancaster*. Some text of the second canto is taken from dog training videos posted on YouTube by McCann Dogs.

Pockets

'You don't have to give masculinity to maleness'
Adedamola said once
and every woman in the room over sixty
fell backwards down the stairs.

(It had been such a hard fucking climb
in those heels –
the handbag so bastard heavy,
all secrets and lipsticks,
       Popsocks,
              Panty Girdles,
                     Eyelash curlers,
                       Epilators,
                           Hairnets,
                           Perfume bottles,
                           Discrete Kleenex,
                               Emergency condoms,

and the rest.

The women
flung arms wide
their faces crumpled with the sudden knowledge
of how this one sentence
shouted down from the top
a long time back
could have saved them the bother,

left their hands free
to put into their own pockets,
swagger to the bar alone
and order a goddamn whiskey).

Whales at night

It is ninety-seven percent water here
and all of it is just slightly too cold
so that every day starts with a small catch of breath
and a gesture towards the belly.

The water is clear and very deep.
In some parts great rollers plough furrows and
stack up as cliffs of glass.

The land is one small crop of smooth old rock
and a single beech tree
whose young leaves are tender and
bitter
and fit into the roof of the mouth.

There is a full moon most nights
except for when the whales rise
turning their massive soft bodies in the waters
lowing
curved into the dark blue horizon

stars dropping onto their wet skins
like moths
like fingernails.

Under

when I wake
tangled in weeds
or the absence of you

I remember
I can breathe under water
the amphibian part
uncurls in murky cortex
loops his tail 'o'

pushes me
web-toed into the depths

I fill my lungs with liquid
the weight of it

inside me
frogspawning
into gelatinous
comfort saltwater
transformed

solid and teeming
we lie in the dark

our solar plexus
busy with

new life
our drowning self
learning to go
down
beyond the light

where gills open
and old limbs
fall away

Sun-return

A bonfire and you laughing
your way through Light my Candle – knowing
all of Rent by heart and later
you burn much brighter than the candle
by the bath for which you have no lighter
it turns out.
These points in darkness –
how we give out what it is we have
by heart, how we return
embers to each other
in the night.

The river slides through a dusk
where we walk in parks
pouring champagne into the ground
holding a lit screen
aloft as if conjuring new deities
for our own church – not just
us two but a congregation scattered
in twilight – across
a city where in the morning
light falls on a vase of yellow roses
gives old name ghosts the heave ho
slakes us with sunshine
shows us, as we fuck
our way through every
gender that there is,
that all of them
are also made of light.

I beg you.
Place me gently in the earth
with tulips at my feet
and lay your body down on mine
and let me grow through you,
with you tilth and loam and through me, you;
to be born again

into the tender petalled
sun return
Light
Light
Light
and all opening to you.
All opening.

Acknowledgements

For Mary Frith and all the unruly dead.

With love and thanks to Adedamola, Am, David, Mallin and Timothy.